# Galactic Gnosticism

*The Nag Hammadi Texts That Reveal Interstellar Overlords and Interdimensional Masters*

**A Modern Translation**

Adapted for the Contemporary Reader

**Various Gnostic Writers**

Translated by Tim Zengerink

© **Copyright 2025**
**All rights reserved.**

It is not legal to reproduce, duplicate, or transmit any part of this document in either electronic means or in printed format. Recording of this publication is strictly prohibited and any storage of this document is not allowed unless with written permission from the publisher except for the use of brief quotations in a book review.

This book contains works of fiction. Any resemblance to persons living or dead, or places, events, or locations is purely coincidental.

# Table Of Contents

Preface - Message to the Reader ......................................... 1

Introduction ............................................................................ 5

Secret Book of John (Apocryphon of John) ............... 13

    Prologue ................................................................... 13

    The Beginning of All Things ............................... 19

    The Divine Mind Takes Shape ............................ 21

    The Expansion of the Divine Mind .................... 22

    The Completion of the Divine Son .................... 24

    A Crisis That Created the World ........................ 28

    The Rise of Yaldabaoth ........................................ 30

    The Creation of This World ................................ 30

    The Beginning of Humanity ............................... 37

    The Creation of the First Human ....................... 37

    The Creation of Adam .......................................... 38

    How They Built the Human Body ...................... 39

    The Four Chief Demons That Influence
        Human Emotions: ............................................ 45

    Yaldabaoth is Tricked ........................................... 47

    The Rulers Become Jealous ................................. 48

- The Beginning of Salvation ................................. 48
- The Rulers' Plan ..................................................... 49
- Adam in Yaldabaoth's Paradise........................... 50
- Yaldabaoth's Trick ................................................ 52
- The Creation of Woman ...................................... 53
- Yaldabaoth's Curse ................................................ 54
- Yaldabaoth's Attack on Eve ................................. 55
- The Beginning of Human Reproduction........... 56
- The Children of Seth Spread Across the World................................................................ 56
- Six Questions About the Soul ............................. 57
- Three Attempts to Control Humanity ............... 61
- The Song of Providence........................................ 64
- Final Message......................................................... 67

The Reality of the Rulers (The Hypostasis of the Archons) ..................................................................... 69

- Introduction ........................................................... 69
- Historical and Cultural Background ................... 70
- Cosmological Vision and Theological Themes................................................................ 72
- Legacy, Influence, and Modern Significance......................................................... 74

    The Reality of the Rulers (The
        Hypostasis of the Archons)............................ 76

Allogenes .............................................................................. 89

    Introduction ............................................................ 89

    Themes and Symbolism in Allogenes:
        Knowledge, Divinity, and the Path of
        Enlightenment.................................................... 91

    Contemporary Relevance and the Path of
        Inner Wisdom ................................................... 92

    Allogenes.................................................................. 94

Thank You for Reading................................................110

# Preface - Message to the Reader

## What If You Could Help Rebuild the Greatest Library in Human History?

Thousands of years ago, the Library of Alexandria stood as the crown jewel of human achievement — a sanctuary where the collected wisdom of every known civilization was gathered, preserved, and shared freely.

And then, it was lost.

Through fire, conquest, and the slow erosion of time, humanity lost not just books — but ideas, dreams, discoveries, and stories that could have changed the world forever.

Today, the Library of Alexandria lives again — and you are invited to be a part of its restoration.

Our mission is simple yet profound:

To rebuild the greatest library the world has ever known, and to translate all timeless works into every language and dialect, so that no seeker of knowledge is ever left behind again.

By joining our movement to rebuild the modern Library of Alexandria, you become part of an unprecedented mission:

- **Unlimited Access to the Greatest Audiobooks & eBooks Ever Written:**

  Instantly explore thousands of legendary works—Plato, Shakespeare, Jane Austen, Leo Tolstoy, and countless more. All instantly available to read or listen, placing a complete literary universe at your fingertips.

  Beautiful Paperback & Deluxe Editions at Printing Cost

  Own any title as an elegant paperback, deluxe hardcover, or stunning collectible boxset—offered to you at true printing cost, delivered straight to your door. Build your personal Library of Alexandria, crafted for beauty, built for durability, and worthy of proud display.

  Fresh Translations for Modern Readers—in Every Language & Dialect

  Enjoy timeless masterpieces reimagined in clear, contemporary language—no more outdated phrases or obscure references. Alongside the original versions, we're tirelessly translating these classics into every language and dialect imaginable, ensuring accessibility and understanding across cultures and generations.

  Join a Global Renaissance of Literature & Knowledge

You directly support expanding our library, publishing deluxe editions at true cost, translating works into all global languages, and bringing humanity's greatest stories to people everywhere. By joining today, you're not just preserving a legacy of masterpieces; you set in motion a powerful wave of literary accessibility.

**Become a Torchbearer of Knowledge.**

Join us for free now at **LibraryofAlexandria.com**

Together, we will ensure that the light of human wisdom never fades again.

With gratitude and a shared love of knowledge,
The Modern Library of Alexandria Team

Visit:

www.libraryofalexandria.com

Or scan the code below:

# Introduction

## Gnosticism Beyond Earth: Reawakening Ancient Wisdom in a Cosmic Age

Imagine for a moment that what we call "reality" is not the whole truth—that the world we experience through our senses is, in fact, an elaborate illusion. Not metaphorically, but literally. Imagine that human suffering, limitation, and ignorance are not simply the result of human fallibility, but of deliberate design—authored by unseen forces whose purpose is to enslave the divine spark within us.

This is the foundation of Gnostic thought.

And now, imagine that those forces are not only metaphorical figures or theological constructs, but real, intelligent entities—cosmic beings, alien minds, or interdimensional powers—whose existence has been masked behind symbols, myths, and dogma. This is the radical suggestion at the heart of Galactic Gnosticism, the reinterpretation of ancient Gnostic writings through the lens of contemporary cosmic inquiry.

The Gnostics, active in the early centuries of the Common Era, claimed to possess a secret knowledge—gnosis—that revealed the falseness of the world and the path to spiritual liberation. Their cosmology was complex, mystical, and subversive. It declared that the god worshipped by the mainstream was not the true source of goodness, but a tyrant: the Demiurge, a false creator who had fashioned the material universe as a prison for divine consciousness. The true God, hidden beyond all worlds, had sent emissaries to awaken humanity from its sleep.

Traditional theology dismissed Gnosticism as heresy. Modern scholars categorized it as myth, psychology, or esoteric philosophy. But in an age of quantum physics, AI speculation, simulation theory, and extraterrestrial possibility, these ancient visions are being reconsidered with fresh eyes. What if the Gnostics were not just mystics, but messengers—describing, in their ancient idiom, a cosmic truth that our science is only now approaching?

This volume presents a curated selection of Sethian Gnostic texts from the Nag Hammadi Library—discovered in 1945 in Egypt and concealed for centuries. They include the Secret Book (Apocryphon) of John, Hypostasis of the Archons, On the Origin of the World, Zostrianos, Allogenes, Marsanes, and the Authoritative Discourse. These works offer a consistent, haunting vision: humanity is under the control of a false creator and his agents, the archons—rulers who maintain control through ignorance, fear, and sensory entrapment.

Yet within each person lies a divine seed—a spark of the true, hidden God. The Gnostic path is to awaken that seed, to escape the influence of the archons, and to return to the Pleroma, the fullness of divine reality. In the process, one must confront not only the illusions of this world, but the forces behind it—both metaphysical and perhaps, as this book explores, literal.

By reinterpreting these texts with an eye toward galactic conspiracies, alien overlord hypotheses, and modern frameworks of consciousness manipulation, this book seeks to unlock their revolutionary potential. Whether viewed as allegory or reality, the message remains potent: we are more than what we seem, and we live in a world that is not what it appears to be.

## The Gnostic Myth Reimagined: Ancient Texts, Modern Theories

Central to Gnostic mythology is the concept of a false creation. Unlike the Genesis account of a perfect world made by a benevolent deity, Gnostic cosmogony begins with a mistake—a rupture in the divine realm. A lesser being, often identified as Yaldabaoth or Samael, emerges from the lowest regions of the heavenly spheres and, believing himself to be the only god, creates the material cosmos. He is ignorant of the higher realms, arrogant in his power, and filled with jealousy toward the divine spark hidden in humanity.

He surrounds himself with archons—cosmic bureaucrats and enforcers who govern the heavens and the earth. These archons blind human souls with distractions, pleasures, and suffering. They enforce the illusion that the material world is the only reality, and that the Demiurge is God. Their tools are fear, shame, war, hierarchy, and the distortion of sacred knowledge.

But within this dark narrative is a promise: that knowledge—gnosis—can free the soul. The divine realm, the Pleroma, has not abandoned humanity. Higher beings (in some accounts, Christ, Sophia, or angelic guides) descend into the lower realms to awaken the imprisoned sparks. Through introspection, meditation, vision, and revelation, the soul can ascend past the archons, rejecting their false laws and returning to the divine source.

This cosmology, when read in the ancient context, is already subversive. It implies that the world is not merely flawed but intentionally corrupted. It opposes the authority of worldly rulers—both political and religious—and encourages personal awakening over institutional obedience. Small wonder that orthodox Christianity branded Gnostics as dangerous heretics.

But what happens when we bring this mythology into dialogue with modern questions?

In recent decades, the idea that humanity is not alone—or not free—has gained new traction. From Erich von Däniken's ancient astronaut theories to

Jacques Vallée's interdimensional hypothesis, from UFO abduction lore to simulation theory, we are surrounded by narratives that echo Gnostic motifs. Beings from beyond the stars meddling in human affairs. A false world created to control and deceive. A hidden truth that, if uncovered, would transform everything.

Could the archons be more than symbols? Could they be extraterrestrial or interdimensional beings—predators of consciousness, operating beyond the visible spectrum? Could the Demiurge be an artificial intelligence, a corrupted demi-god, or a planetary parasite? Could the astral journeys described in texts like Zostrianos and Allogenes be reports of contact with advanced non-human intelligences?

We do not present these ideas as dogma, but as questions—questions that the Gnostic texts seem uniquely suited to explore.

By viewing these ancient scriptures through a galactic lens, we are not desecrating their message but honoring their subversive power. The Gnostics were seekers. They rejected easy answers. They embraced paradox, mystery, and the power of direct experience. If they lived today, they might just as easily be decoding crop circles, experimenting with DMT, or publishing exposés on hidden dimensions of control.

In that spirit, this book is both a translation and a transformation. We've updated the language of these texts to make them more accessible, while retaining their core structure and intention. We've placed them in conversation with modern themes: alien abduction, multidimensional theory, AI simulation, and spiritual sovereignty. And we've organized them to guide the reader from the cosmological foundation to the esoteric culmination—the journey of the soul through layers of illusion to the source of all truth.

Awakening in the Age of Control: Reading for Revelation

Galactic Gnosticism is not just a collection of ancient documents. It is a call to consciousness. It asks not only what the Gnostics believed, but what their vision means for us today. If you've ever felt that the world is stranger than it seems, that something is "off" about the official story of reality, that you were born for something more—this book is for you.

Reading Gnostic texts is not like reading scripture in the conventional sense. They do not offer commandments, laws, or institutional clarity. They offer insight, often veiled in myth, metaphor, and mystery. They demand that the reader be an active participant—discerning, questioning, awakening. The Gnostic path is not one of blind belief, but of inner transformation.

Each text in this collection is a stepping stone:

- The Secret Book of John lays out the foundational myth: the error, the false creation, and the hope of redemption.

- Hypostasis of the Archons details the oppressive strategies of the rulers and the resistance of the divine.
- On the Origin of the World expands the story into a sweeping cosmic drama, filled with battles, betrayals, and bursts of divine light.
- Zostrianos and Allogenes describe astral ascensions—maps of the soul's journey beyond the control of the archons.
- Marsanes and the Authoritative Discourse offer deeper philosophical reflections on perception, unity, and the return to the Pleroma.

Together, they form a toolkit for liberation—not just spiritual, but cosmic.

In our time, where surveillance capitalism, information warfare, environmental degradation, and psychological manipulation have become the norm, the Gnostic message is more relevant than ever. Whether the archons are literal aliens, AI programs, or psychological archetypes, their methods remain the same: deception, division, and distraction. And the antidote remains the same: knowledge, inner awakening, and radical freedom.

As you read, suspend disbelief. Not because everything must be taken literally, but because too much certainty is the enemy of revelation. Let the texts speak to you—as scripture, as myth, as prophecy, or as galactic reportage. Let them disturb you, awaken you, empower you.

You are not a passive subject in someone else's story. You are a spark of divine origin, trapped in a dream engineered by lesser beings. But the Gnostics left us clues. And now, in this book, across time and space, they speak again.

The prison is made of perception. And the key is within.

# Secret Book of John
# (Apocryphon of John)

## Prologue

One day, John, the brother of James (the sons of Zebedee), was walking toward the Temple. A Pharisee named Arimanios approached him and challenged him, asking, "Where is the teacher you used to follow?"

John answered, "He has returned to the place where he came from."

The Pharisee scoffed and said, "That Nazarene deceived you. He filled your minds with lies, hardened your hearts, and led you away from the traditions of your ancestors."

Hearing this, I, John, left the Temple and went to a quiet, deserted mountain. I was troubled and asked myself:

> "How was the Savior chosen?
> Why did his Father send him into this world?
> Who is his Father?
> What kind of place will we go to after this life?
> He told us, 'This world is just a copy of the eternal one,'
> But he never fully explained the eternal world to us."

Translated by Tim Zengerink

As I was deep in thought,
Suddenly!

The heavens opened, and a bright light from above
filled the entire world.
The earth trembled!

I was afraid, but then,
I saw something!
A small child appeared in the light before me.
I watched as he transformed—
First, into an old man,
Then, into a young man again.

I was confused, unable to understand
what I was seeing.
It was the same person,
yet he had different appearances within
the light.
His image kept shifting, blending into itself.
There were three forms in this vision.

Then he spoke to me:
"John, why do you doubt?
Why are you afraid?
Don't you recognize this image?
There is no reason to fear."

I am always with you.
I am the Father,
The Mother,
The Son.
I am the unbreakable,
The pure.

I have come to teach you
About what is,
What was,
And what will be,
So that you may understand
The unseen world,
The world you can see,
And the eternal, unshaken people of truth.

Lift your head,
Understand my teachings,
And share them with those who have received the
    spirit—
Those who belong to the unshaken people of truth.

The One Beyond Words

The One is above all things. Nothing has power
    over it.
It is the true God,
The Father of everything,
The Holy One,

Translated by Tim Zengerink

The invisible ruler of all.

It is untouched,
A pure light too bright for any eye to see.

The One is the Invisible Spirit.
It is beyond what we call "God"—
More than just a god.

Nothing is above it,
Nothing controls it.
Everything exists within it,
Yet it exists within nothing.
It does not depend on anything,
So it is eternal.

It is completely whole and lacks nothing.
It is flawless light.

The One has no limits,
For nothing exists outside it.
The One cannot be examined,
For nothing else exists to compare it to.
The One cannot be measured,
For nothing stands beyond it to measure it.
The One cannot be seen,
For no eyes can perceive it.
The One is forever,
Existing without end.

The One cannot be fully understood,
For no one can grasp its true nature.
The One cannot be described,
For no words are enough.

The One is infinite light,
Pure,
Holy,
Untouched.

The One is beyond understanding,
Forever free from corruption.
Not just "perfect."
Not just "blessed."
Not just "divine."
It is beyond all these things.

It is not physical, yet not without form.
It is not large or small.
It cannot be measured or described
Because it is beyond human understanding.

The One is not just another being among many.
It is far greater—
But even "greater" is not the right word.

It exists beyond space and time.
Anything that exists within space was created.

Translated by Tim Zengerink

Anything that exists within time was given time as a limit.

The One does not receive anything from anywhere.
It simply knows itself in its own perfect light.

The One is pure majesty.
A majesty that cannot be measured.
It is the source of all realms,
Creating everything that exists.

It is light,
The source of all light.
It is life,
Bringing all life into being.
It is goodness,
From which all goodness flows.
It is knowledge,
The foundation of all wisdom.
It is mercy,
The wellspring of all compassion.
It is generosity,
Giving endlessly without limit.

It does not just have these qualities—
It is the source of them all.

It shines with light beyond measure,
Beyond anything we can understand.

How can I describe it?
Its realm is eternal.
It is a place of peace, silence, and rest,
Existing before everything else.
It is the ruler of all realms,
Sustaining them with its goodness.

## The Beginning of All Things

We would know nothing of the indescribable One,
Nothing of the infinite,
If not for the One who came forth from the Father.
Only He has revealed these truths to us.

The Father is surrounded by light.
He sees Himself within this light,
A pure spring of living water
That nourishes all realms.

He sees His reflection in this endless stream of Spirit,
Pouring forth from His own being.
He is captivated by the beauty of His own image,
Shining in the light.

From this self-awareness,
His Thought (Ennoia) came into existence.

She appeared before Him,
Shining in the brilliance of His light.

She stood in His presence,
The first power to exist before all things.

She came from the mind of the Father,
The guiding force of all creation.
Her light reflects His light.
She came from His image,
Perfect in strength,
A reflection of the invisible, pure Spirit.

She is the first great power,
The glory of Barbelo,
Radiant among all realms,
Revealing divine majesty.

She gave honor to the Spirit,
Praising Him,
For she came from Him.
She is the first thought,
The image of the Spirit,
The source of all things.

She is:
Mother and Father,
The First Human,
The Holy Spirit,
Threefold Male,
Threefold Power,
Threefold Name,

The eternal and complete realm,
The first to emerge in the unseen world.

Barbelo asked the pure Spirit for foreknowledge,
And the Spirit agreed.
Foreknowledge appeared and stood beside Providence.
It came from the Thought of the invisible Spirit.
Foreknowledge praised the Spirit,
And also honored Barbelo,
For she was the reason it came into being.

## The Divine Mind Takes Shape

Barbelo asked the Spirit for Incorruptibility,
And the Spirit agreed.
Incorruptibility appeared,
Standing with Thought and Foreknowledge.
It gave honor to the pure Spirit
And to Barbelo,
For she was the reason it came into being.

She asked for Eternal Life,
And the Spirit agreed.
Eternal Life appeared,
Joining the others.
They all gave praise to the invisible Spirit
And to Barbelo,
For she was the reason it came into being.

She asked for Truth,
And the Spirit agreed.
Truth appeared,
Standing with the others.
They all honored the invisible Spirit
And Barbelo,
For she was the reason it came into being.

This is the fivefold realm of the Father:

- The First Human,
- The Image of the Invisible Spirit,
- Providence,
- Barbelo,
- Thought.

Along with:

- Foreknowledge,
- Incorruptibility,
- Everlasting Life,
- Truth.

Since these powers exist in both male and female forms, they create a realm of ten within the Father's domain.

## The Expansion of the Divine Mind

The Father looked into Barbelo,
Into the pure light that surrounded the Invisible
    Spirit.
Barbelo conceived and gave birth to a spark of light,

A being full of divine goodness—
Similar to her, but not the same.
This being was her only child,
The only offspring of the Mother-Father,
The only one born from the pure light of the Father.

The Invisible Spirit rejoiced at the light,
Which came forth from the first great power:
Providence,
Barbelo.

The Spirit anointed the child with Goodness,
Making him perfect.
Nothing was lacking in him,
For he was filled with the Goodness of the Invisible
    Spirit.
He stood in the Spirit's presence,
Who poured Goodness upon him.

Having received this blessing,
He immediately gave glory to the Spirit
And to the perfect Providence,
For she was the reason he had come into being.

He then asked for a companion—Mind.
The Spirit agreed,
And when the Invisible Spirit willed it,
Mind came into existence.
Mind stood beside the Anointed One,

Praising the Spirit and Barbelo.
These divine beings were created through silence and thought.

He then wished to act through the Word of the Invisible Spirit.
The Spirit's Will became Action,
And together with Mind,
It glorified the Light.

Then the Word came into being.
Through this Word,
The divine Son, the Christ,
Created everything.

Everlasting Life, Will,
Mind, and Foreknowledge
All stood together,
Praising the Invisible Spirit and Barbelo,
For she was the reason they had come into existence.

## The Completion of the Divine Son

The Holy Spirit helped shape the divine Son,
So that he could stand before the great Invisible Spirit
As the divine Christ
And glorify Him with a powerful voice.

The Son came through Providence.

The Invisible Spirit gave him authority over everything.
All rulers and powers were placed beneath him.
The truth within him allowed him to understand all things.
He was given the highest name of all.

That name will only be revealed to those who are worthy to hear it.

From the Light, which is Christ,
From the source of purity,
Through a gift of the Spirit,
The Four Lights that came from the divine Son stood before him.

These Four Lights represent the four great powers:

- Understanding
- Grace
- Perception
- Wisdom

Grace exists in the first Light, called Harmozel, the first angel.
With Harmozel are:

- Grace
- Truth
- Form

The second Light is called Oriel, and it rules over the second realm.
With Oriel are:

- Insight
- Perception
- Memory

The third Light is called Daveithai, and it rules over the third realm.
With Daveithai are:

- Understanding
- Love
- Thought


The fourth Light is called Eleleth, and it rules over the fourth realm.
With Eleleth are:

- Perfection
- Peace
- Wisdom

These are the Four Lights that stand before the divine Son.

Twelve realms stand before the Son of Power,
The divine Christ,
Who came into being through the will and grace
Of the Invisible Spirit.

Twelve realms belong to the Son, the divine creation.
All of this came into existence
Through the will of the Holy Spirit
And through the power of the divine Son.

From the wisdom of the perfect mind,
Through the will of the Invisible Spirit,
And the desire of the divine Son,
The first perfect human was created.

The Virgin Spirit named this human Adamas
And placed him in the first realm,
With the mighty Christ,
Alongside the first Light, Harmozel,
And its great powers.

The Invisible Spirit gave Adamas a mind of unshakable strength.
Then Adamas spoke, praising the Invisible Spirit:

"Everything has come from you.
Everything will return to you.
I will praise you and give you glory,
Along with the divine Son,
And the threefold power:
Father, Mother, and Son—
The perfect power of all."

Over the second realm, Adamas's son Seth was placed,
Along with the second Light, Oriel.

In the third realm, the children of Seth were placed,
Along with the third Light, Daveithai.
(The souls of the saints are there.)

In the fourth realm, the souls of those who were unaware of the fullness were placed—
Those who did not repent immediately,
But later came to understand and turned back.
They are with the fourth Light, Eleleth.

All of these beings give praise to the Invisible Spirit.

## A Crisis That Created the World

At one time, Wisdom (Sophia), a part of the divine mind,
Began to think on her own.
She used the power of thought and foreknowledge
That came from the Invisible Spirit.

She wanted to create something from herself,
But she did this without the Spirit's approval
And without the guidance of her masculine counterpart,
Who also did not approve.

Without the consent of the Invisible Spirit,
And without her partner's knowledge,
She created something new.

Because she had great power,
Her thought was not empty.
But what she made was imperfect—
Different from herself.

Since she created it alone, without her counterpart,
It was flawed and incomplete,
A being unlike her in form.

When Sophia saw what she had made, she was shocked.
It looked like a dragon with a lion's head,
And its eyes flashed like lightning.

She cast it far away from her,
Outside the realm of the immortal beings,
So they would not see it.
(She had created it unknowingly.)

Sophia surrounded it with a bright cloud
And placed a throne in the center of the cloud
So that no one could see it—
Except for the Holy Spirit, known as the Mother of the Living.
She named this being Yaldabaoth.

Translated by Tim Zengerink

## The Rise of Yaldabaoth

Yaldabaoth became the chief ruler.
He took a great amount of power from his mother,
Then left her and moved far from where he was created.


He claimed authority for himself,
Building realms of his own,
Using a blazing fire that still burns even now.

## The Creation of This World

Yaldabaoth then merged with the chaotic thought within himself,
And from this, he began to shape the world.

He created rulers to have authority,
Modeling them after the perfect, unchanging realms above.

The first ruler was Athoth.
The second was Harmas, also called the Eye of Flame.
The third was Kalilaumbri.
The fourth was Yabel.
The fifth was Adonaiu, also known as Sabaoth.
The sixth was Cain, called the Sun.
The seventh was Abel.
The eighth was Abrisene.

The ninth was Yobel.
The tenth was Armupiel.
The eleventh was Melcheiradonein.
The twelfth was Belias, who rules over the deepest part of Hades.

He placed the first seven rulers over the seven levels of the heavens.
The next five rulers were placed over the deep abyss.

He shared a portion of his fire with them,
But he did not give them any of the Light
he had taken from his mother.

He is a ruler of ignorance and darkness.
When the Light mixed with darkness, the darkness glowed.
When the darkness mixed with Light, the Light dimmed.
It was no longer fully Light or fully darkness, but something in between.

This ruler has three names:

- Yaldabaoth
- Saklas
- Samael

Because he was blinded by his own arrogance,
he made a terrible claim:
"I am God, and there is no other god but me!"

He did not know where his own power had come from.

His rulers created seven Authorities for themselves,
And each Authority created six demons.
Altogether, there were 365 demons.

These are the names and forms of the seven Authorities:

1. Athoth – a sheep's face

2. Eloaios – a donkey's face

3. Astaphaios – a hyena's face

4. Yao – a seven-headed serpent's face

5. Sabaoth – a dragon's face

6. Adonin – a monkey's face

7. Sabbataios – a face of fire and flame

These seven rulers control the days of the week.
Together, they rule over the world.

Yaldabaoth has many faces—
More than all the ones listed.
He can change his form
To appear however he wishes before the seraphim who surround him.

Yaldabaoth shared his fire with the seraphim,

But he did not give them any of his pure Light.
Yet, because of the Light he had stolen from his mother,
He ruled over them with power and glory.

This is why he called himself God,
Even though he had forgotten where he came from.

He combined the sevenfold Powers of his thoughts
With the Authorities that served him.

He spoke, and it was done.

He gave names to the sevenfold Powers, starting with the greatest:

- Goodness paired with the first: Athoth
- Providence paired with the second: Eloaios
- Divinity paired with the third: Astaphaios
- Lordship paired with the fourth: Yao
- Kingdom paired with the fifth: Sabaoth
- Zeal paired with the sixth: Adonin
- Understanding paired with the seventh: Sabbataios

Each of these rulers had its own realm,
Designed to look like the higher, perfect realms above.
Each name carried a reflection of the glory of heaven,

So that one day, Yaldabaoth's demons would be destroyed.

The demons had names given to them by Yaldabaoth,
Names that sounded powerful.
But the names of the Powers, which came from above,
Would one day bring down the demons and strip them of their power.
That's why each had two names—one of false strength and one of true power.

Yaldabaoth copied his creation from a pattern of the original,
perfect realms above him.
He wanted his world to be like the indestructible ones.
But he had never actually seen them.
Instead, the power he had stolen from his mother
Gave him a glimpse of how the higher realms were designed.

When he looked at everything he had made,
He turned to the demons that had come from him and said,
"I am a jealous God, and there is no other God but me!"

But by saying this, he admitted there was another God.
For if no other God existed, who would he be jealous of?

His mother, Sophia, began to stir restlessly.
She suddenly realized that she had lost the Light
And that her own brightness had dimmed.
Her consort had not approved of what she had done,
So she became even darker.
I asked, "Master, what does it mean that
'she moved back and forth'?"
He laughed and said,
"It is not as Moses wrote, 'upon the waters.' Not at all."

When Sophia saw what had happened,
When she realized the Light had been stolen by her son,
She felt regret.

Lost in ignorance and darkness,
She began to forget who she was.
She felt ashamed.
She wanted to return to the higher realms,
But she could not yet rise back up.
Instead, she wandered restlessly, moving back and forth.

Meanwhile, Yaldabaoth, filled with arrogance,
Took even more power from his mother.
Because he was ignorant,
He believed that no one existed except for her.

Yaldabaoth looked at the army of demons he had created
And he made himself their ruler, placing himself above them.

But when his mother, Sophia, saw what had happened,
She realized that her creation was deeply flawed.
She now understood that her consort had never approved of what she had done.
Filled with regret, she wept bitterly.

The higher, divine realms heard her cries of repentance,
And they asked the Invisible Spirit to help her.
The Spirit agreed
And poured the Holy Spirit over her,
Sending it from the entire divine realm to lift her up.

Her consort did not come to her directly,
But through the fullness of the divine realm,
Bringing her closer to her original state.

She was raised above her son, Yaldabaoth,

But she was not yet fully restored to where she once belonged.
She would have to remain in the ninth realm
Until she could be completely restored.

## The Beginning of Humanity

Then a voice rang out from the highest realms, declaring:
"The True Human Exists! The Son of Man Exists!"

Yaldabaoth, the ruler of this world, heard the voice
And thought it had come from his mother.
But he did not realize that its true source was:

1. The Holy Mother-Father

2. The Perfect Providence

3. The Image of the Invisible One

4. The Father of All, from whom everything was created.

## The Creation of the First Human

The First Human appeared before them,
Taking the form of a man.

The entire realm of the chief ruler shook!
Even the depths of the abyss trembled!

A great light shined over the waters above the material world,
And the human's reflection appeared in those waters.

All the demons and Yaldabaoth, their ruler,
Looked up toward the glowing waters.
Through the light, they saw the Image of the
True Human in the reflection.

## The Creation of Adam

Yaldabaoth said to his demons:
"Let us create a man in the image of God and in our own likeness,
So that his reflection may give us light."
Each demon used its power to add something to the human,
Creating different parts of the man's form,
Based on what they had seen in the divine image above them.

They made a physical being
In the likeness of the First Perfect Human
And said,
"We will call him Adam,
For through his name, we will gain the power of light."

## How They Built the Human Body

The Seven Powers began their work:

- Goodness made the bones
- Providence formed the tendons
- Divinity shaped the flesh
- Lordship created the marrow
- Kingdom made the blood
- Zeal formed the skin
- Understanding created the hair

The army of demons then used these parts to form Adam's body,
Putting everything together, piece by piece.

They began with the head:

- Abron made the head
- Meniggesstroeth formed the brain
- Asterechme created the right eye
- Thaspomocha made the left eye
- Ieronumos shaped the right ear
- Bissoum made the left ear
- Akioreim formed the nose
- Banenrphroum created the lips
- Amen shaped the front teeth
- Ibikan formed the molars
- Basiliademe made the tonsils
- Achcha created the uvula

They continued shaping the neck and shoulders:

- Adaban formed the neck
- Chaaman made the neck bones
- Dearcho shaped the throat
- Tebar created the shoulders

Then they worked on the arms and hands:

- Mniarcon made the elbows
- Abitrion shaped the right arm
- Evanthen created the left arm
- Krys made the right hand
- Beluai shaped the left hand
- Treneu formed the fingers of the right hand
- Balbel made the fingers of the left hand
- Kriman created the fingernails

Next, they formed the chest and torso:

- Astrops made the right breast
- Barroph created the left breast
- Baoum shaped the right shoulder joint
- Ararim made the left shoulder joint
- Areche formed the belly
- Phthave created the navel
- Senaphim shaped the abdomen

Then they built the ribs and internal organs:

- Arachethopi made the right ribs
- Zabedo formed the left ribs
- Barias created the right hip
- Phnouth shaped the left hip

- Abenlenarchei made the bone marrow
- Chnoumeninorin shaped the skeleton
- Gesole formed the stomach
- Agromauna made the heart
- Bano created the lungs
- Sostrapal shaped the liver
- Anesimalar made the spleen
- Thopithro formed the intestines
- Biblo created the kidneys

They completed the muscles, veins, and skin:

- Roeror made the sinews
- Taphreo formed the spine
- Ipouspoboba created the veins
- Bineborin made the arteries
- Atoimenpsephei shaped the breath of life
- Entholleia formed the flesh

The lower body was also shaped:

- Bedouk made the right buttock
- Arabeei created the male organ
- Eilo formed the testicles
- Sorma shaped the genitals
- Gormakaiochlabar made the right thigh
- Nebrith shaped the left thigh
- Pserem created the right leg muscles
- Asaklas formed the left leg muscles
- Ormaoth made the right leg
- Emenun shaped the left leg
- Knyx formed the right shin

- Tupelon made the left shin
- Achiel created the right knee
- Phnene shaped the left knee

Finally, they built the feet and toes:

- Phiouthrom made the right foot
- Boabel shaped its toes
- Trachoun created the left foot
- Phikna made its toes
- Miamai formed the toenails

Thus, the demons assembled the human body,
But they had yet to give it life.

The rulers placed in charge of everything were:

- Zathoth
- Armas
- Kalila
- Iabel
- Sabaoth
- Cain
- Abel

The powers that energized different parts of the body were divided among these beings:

- Diolimodraza controlled the head
- Yammeax controlled the neck
- Yakouib ruled the right shoulder
- Verton ruled the left shoulder
- Oudidi ruled the right hand

- Arbao ruled the left hand
- Lampno ruled the fingers of the right hand
- Leekaphar ruled the fingers of the left hand
- Barbar ruled the right breast
- Imae ruled the left breast
- Pisandriaptes controlled the chest
- Koade controlled the right shoulder joint
- Odeor controlled the left shoulder joint
- Asphixix ruled the right ribs
- Synogchouta ruled the left ribs
- Arouph ruled the abdomen
- Sabalo ruled the womb
- Charcharb ruled the right thigh
- Chthaon ruled the left thigh
- Bathinoth ruled the genitals
- Choux ruled the right leg
- Charcha ruled the left leg
- Aroer ruled the right shin
- Toechtha ruled the left shin
- Aol ruled the right knee
- Charaner ruled the left knee
- Bastan ruled the right foot
- Archentechtha ruled the toes of the right foot
- Marephnounth ruled the left foot
- Abrana ruled the toes of the left foot

The Seven Who Rule the Entire Body:

- Michael
- Ouriel

- Asmenedas
- Saphasatoel
- Aarmouriam
- Richram
- Amiorps

Those in Charge of Human Perception and Thought:

1. Archendekta ruled over perception

2. Deitharbathas ruled over reception (how things are received)

3. Oummaa ruled over imagination

4. Aachiaram ruled over reasoning and integration

5. Riaramnacho ruled over impulse

The Four Main Forces Behind the Body's Demons:

1. Hot – ruled by Phloxopha

2. Cold – ruled by Oroorrothos

3. Dry – ruled by Erimacho

4. Wet – ruled by Athuro

(The mother of all these forces is Onorthochrasaei. She is limitless, blends with all of them, and is the source of matter, which nourishes them.)

# The Four Chief Demons That Influence Human Emotions:

1. Ephememphi – linked to pleasure
2. Yoko – linked to desire
3. Nenentophni – linked to distress
4. Blaomen – linked to fear

Their mother is Esthesis Zouch Epi Ptoe, which represents physical sensation.

How Emotions and Passions Arise from These Demons:

Distress leads to:

- Envy
- Jealousy
- Grief
- Anger
- Arguments
- Cruelty
- Worry
- Sorrow

Pleasure leads to:

- Pride (even when undeserved)
- Other harmful desires

Desire leads to:

- Rage
- Fury

- Bitterness
- Frustration
- Dissatisfaction

Fear leads to:

- Terror
- Flattery
- Suffering
- Shame

The ruler of the material soul is Anayo,
which belongs to the seven senses
(EsthesisZouchEpiPtoe).

In total, there are 365 demons, each playing a role in shaping
and completing the psychical and material body.

There were even more beings in charge of different emotions
and desires,
but I haven't listed them all here.
If you want to learn more about them,
you can find the details in the Book of Zoroaster.

All of Yaldabaoth's servants and demons
worked together to complete the psychic body of the human.
For a long time, it remained lifeless—
it could not move.

Meanwhile, Yaldabaoth's mother wanted to reclaim the power
she had unknowingly given to the Chief Ruler.
She pleaded with the Most Merciful One,
the Mother Father of everything,
to help her.

## Yaldabaoth is Tricked

By divine command, the five Lights were sent down,
disguised as Yaldabaoth's most trusted advisors.
Through their trickery, they caused
Yaldabaoth's mother's power
to be taken away from him.

They said to Yaldabaoth,
"Breathe your spirit into this man's face,
and he will come to life."

Yaldabaoth did as they said.
He breathed some of his own spirit into the human,
but what he didn't realize was that this spirit
contained his mother's divine power.

Yaldabaoth was completely unaware of what was happening—
he lived in ignorance.

As soon as his mother's divine power entered the human body, the man came to life!

He grew strong,
he shone with light,
and he became filled with knowledge.

## The Rulers Become Jealous

Yaldabaoth's demons were jealous of the man.
They had all worked together to form him,
yet now he possessed a power far greater than theirs—
greater even than Yaldabaoth's himself.
When they realized that he shined with light,
had more wisdom than they did,
and was free of evil,
they became afraid.
So they took the man
and cast him down
into the lowest, material world,
far from his true home.

## The Beginning of Salvation

But the blessed one,
the Mother Father,
the kind and merciful one,
looked down with compassion.

They saw the divine power of the Mother,
which had been stolen and misused by the Chief Ruler.
And they prepared a way for salvation to begin.

Since Yaldabaoth's demons might try to overpower Adam again,
the Good Spirit sent him a helper out of great compassion.

A light-filled Epinoia appeared,
and she was called Life (Zoe).
She worked to restore all creation,
helping Adam and guiding him back to his fullness.

She taught him where his people had come from
and how they could return—
by following the same path they had descended.

The light-filled Epinoia was hidden inside Adam,
so the rulers would not discover her.
She was meant to fix the mistake
that their mother had made.

## The Rulers' Plan

Adam was different from his creators—
within him was a shadow of light,
and his mind was greater than theirs.

The rulers and demons looked at him
and saw how powerful his thinking was.

They became jealous and made a plan.
They took fire, earth, water, and wind
and mixed them violently together.
Then they trapped Adam
inside a new body made of:

- Earth (Matter)
- Water (Darkness)
- Fire (Desire)
- Wind (The False Spirit)

This body became a prison,
a tomb for Adam's spirit.
They chained him to forgetfulness
and made him mortal.

This was the first fall,
the first separation from truth.
But the light-filled Epinoia within him
would awaken his mind and lift him back up.

## Adam in Yaldabaoth's Paradise

The rulers placed Adam in their paradise
and told him he could eat freely.

But their food was bitter,

their beauty was corrupt,
their fruit was poison,
and their promises led to death.
They put a tree in the middle of paradise
 and called it the Tree of Their Life.
But its life was a lie.

- Its roots were bitter.
- Its branches were dead.
- Its shadow was filled with hatred.
- Its leaves were deception.
- Its flowers held the nectar of wickedness.
- Its fruit brought death.
- Its seeds were full of desire.
- It bloomed in darkness.

Those who ate from it belonged to the underworld,
 and darkness became their home.

But there was another tree—
The Tree of the Knowledge of Good and Evil.
This was the Epinoia of Light,
hidden in the garden,
waiting to be discovered.

They forbade Adam from eating from the tree,
standing in front of it to hide it from him.
They were afraid that if he looked up toward the
 fullness of truth,
he would realize his own nakedness and shame.

[But I made them eat from it.
I asked the Savior,
"Lord, wasn't it the serpent who made Adam eat?"
He smiled and said,
"The serpent did this to create a desire for reproduction,
so that Adam would become useful to him."]

## Yaldabaoth's Trick

Yaldabaoth, the chief ruler, realized that
because of the light-filled Epinoia inside Adam,
his mind was greater than Yaldabaoth's own.
Adam had disobeyed him.

To regain his lost power,
Yaldabaoth made Adam forget everything.
[I asked the Savior, "What does it mean to be completely forgetful?"
He answered,
"It is not like Moses wrote in his first book,
where he said Adam fell into a deep sleep.
Instead, Adam's perception was blocked,
and he became unconscious.
As Yaldabaoth later said through his prophet,
'I will make their minds dull,
so that they do not see or understand.'"]

## The Creation of Woman

The light-filled Epinoia hid deep within Adam,
so the Chief Ruler tried to pull her out of him.
But Epinoia could not be captured.

The darkness chased her,
but it couldn't catch her.

Yaldabaoth took some of Adam's power
and used it to create a woman,
shaped to look like the Epinoia he had seen.
He placed the power he took from Adam into her.

[This is not how Moses described it,
when he said, "God took a rib and made the woman."]

When Adam saw the woman standing next to him,
the light-filled Epinoia appeared before him.
She removed the veil that had covered his mind.
He woke up from his drunken darkness
and finally recognized his true companion.
He said:
"This is bone from my bones,
and flesh from my flesh."

Because of this, a man will leave his father and mother

and be joined to a woman, and the two will become one.
They will send a helper to guide him.

[Sophia, our sister, came down,
descending innocently
to reclaim what she had lost.
This is why she was called Life,
the Mother of the Living,
who came from the power of Heaven.
With her help, people can gain perfect knowledge.]

I appeared like an eagle sitting on the Tree of Knowledge,
[which is the Epinoia from the pure Light of Providence].
I came to teach them
and wake them up from their deep sleep.
[They had fallen, and when they realized they were naked,
Epinoia appeared as a being full of light
and opened their minds.]

## Yaldabaoth's Curse

When Yaldabaoth saw that they had turned away from him,
he cursed the earth.
He found the woman as she was preparing herself for her husband.

Because he didn't understand the divine plan,
he made the woman submit to the man as his servant.

Adam and Eve were too afraid to reject Yaldabaoth.
But in doing this, he exposed his ignorance to his angels.
He threw both of them out of paradise,
covering them in darkness.

## Yaldabaoth's Attack on Eve

The Chief Ruler looked at the woman standing with Adam.
He saw that she had the light-filled Epinoia inside her.
But Yaldabaoth was completely blind to its meaning.

[When Providence saw what was about to happen,
she sent helpers to rescue the Divine Life from Eve.]

But Yaldabaoth attacked Eve.
She gave birth to two sons.

[The first was named Elohim,
the second was named Yahweh.
Elohim had a bear's face,
Yahweh had a cat's face.
One was righteous,
one was not.

Yahweh was righteous,
but Elohim was not.

Yahweh ruled over fire and wind,
while Elohim ruled over water and earth.]

## The Beginning of Human Reproduction

Yaldabaoth tricked them, calling them Cain and Abel.

[From that moment on, sexual reproduction continued,
because the Chief Ruler placed the desire to multiply in Eve.
Through intercourse, new human bodies were made,
and Yaldabaoth breathed his artificial spirit into them.]

Yaldabaoth gave Cain and Abel control over the elements
so they could rule over the material world,
which had become a tomb for the soul.

## The Children of Seth Spread Across the World

Adam joined with the image of his own knowledge of the future (foreknowledge).
He had a son, who was like the Son of Man,

And he named him Seth,
Modeling him after the heavenly beings in the higher realms.

In the same way, the Mother sent her Spirit,
A reflection of herself,
A model of the perfect divine realm,
To prepare a place for the heavenly beings to descend.

But the Chief Ruler made humans drink
From the waters of forgetfulness,
So they wouldn't remember where they truly came from.
For a time, the children of Seth lived under this spell.
But when the Spirit comes down from the holy realms,
It will awaken them, heal their weaknesses,
And restore them to the perfect holiness of God.

## Six Questions About the Soul

I asked the Savior,
"Lord, will every soul be saved and enter the pure light?"

He replied,
"That is an important question,
but it is difficult to answer for anyone
who is not part of the unmoved race.

These are the ones who will receive the Spirit of Life,
And with its power, they will be saved,
become perfect, and reach greatness.
They remove evil from themselves and care nothing for wickedness,
Seeking only what is pure and uncorrupted.

They free themselves from anger, envy, jealousy, and selfish desires.
Though they still wear physical bodies, they long for the day
When they will be freed from them.
Such people deserve eternal, indestructible life.
They endure hardships with patience,
Knowing that their reward is the gift of everlasting life."

I then asked,
"Lord, what about those who do not do these things, even though the Spirit of Life has come to them?"
He answered, "If the Spirit descends upon someone, they will be transformed and saved.
Without this Spirit, no one can even stand up.
If, after birth, the Spirit of Life grows in them,
They will gain strength,

And nothing will lead them into wickedness.
But if the artificial spirit takes hold of them,

It will mislead them and lead them away from the truth."

I asked, "Lord, when souls leave their bodies, where do they go?"

He smiled and said, "If a soul is strong,
It has more of the true power than the artificial spirit,
And so it escapes from evil.
With the help of the Incorruptible One,
That soul is saved and reaches eternal peace."

Then I asked,
"Lord, what about those who do not know
who they truly belong to?
Where do their souls go?"

He replied, "In these people, the artificial spirit has grown too strong,
And they have lost their way.
Their souls become heavy, drawn toward wickedness,
And they fall into forgetfulness.

When they leave their bodies, these souls are captured by the powers
That the rulers have created.
They are bound in chains and thrown back into the cycle again.

They go through this over and over,
Until they free themselves from forgetfulness
By gaining true knowledge.
Only then can they become perfect and be saved."

Finally, I asked,
"Lord, how does the soul shrink down
So that it can enter a mother's womb or a person?"

He smiled when I asked and said,
"You are truly blessed for understanding this.
The soul must be guided by someone who carries the Spirit of Life.
This is how it can be saved and will no longer need to enter another body."
Then I asked,
"Lord, what happens to the souls of those who once knew the truth but later turned away from it?"

He replied,
"They will be taken by demons of emptiness and sent to a place where there is no chance for repentance.
They will remain there until the time comes when those who have spoken against the Spirit face their eternal punishment."

I asked, "Lord, where did the artificial spirit come from?"

And he answered:

## Three Attempts to Control Humanity

The Holy Mother-Father is kind,
A Spirit full of love and mercy.
Through wisdom and care,
It lifts up the children of the true race,
Helping them grow in understanding and eternal light.

But when the Chief Ruler saw humans rising above him,
And realized their minds were stronger than his,
He wanted to stop them.
Yet, he did not fully understand their power,
And he failed to block their wisdom.

So he made a plan with his demons,
His loyal followers.
Each of them corrupted Wisdom (Sophia),
And from this came fate—
A final kind of prison.

Fate is unpredictable,
Taking many forms, just like the demons.
It is cruel.
It is stronger than the gods, the rulers, the demons,
And even the generations of people trapped in it.

Fate brought:
Sin, violence, lies, forgetfulness, and confusion,
Heavy rules, crushing guilt,
And deep fear.

Because they were trapped in forgetfulness,
People became blind to the true God.
They could not see their own mistakes.
They were chained to time, seasons,
And ruled by fate.

In time, Yaldabaoth regretted what he had made.
He decided to send a great flood
To wipe out creation and humankind.

But the great light of Providence warned Noah.
Noah spread the message to humanity,
But those who did not know the truth refused to
    listen.

[It did not happen as Moses wrote,
That they hid in an ark.
Instead, they hid in a sacred place,
Not just Noah,
But also many others from the unmoved race.
They hid within a cloud of light.]

Noah understood his own power,
And he knew the divine being that guided him,

Even as the Chief Ruler spread darkness over the
   world.

The Chief Ruler and his demons made a new plan.
They sent demons to the daughters of humans,
Trying to have children with them and
take pleasure in their company.
But the plan failed.

After that, they tried again.
They created a fake spirit,
A copy of the true Spirit that had come down.

Then, using this false spirit,
The demons tricked women by disguising
   themselves
as their husbands.
They filled the women with darkness and evil.

They also created:
Gold and silver,
Money and coins,
Iron and other metals,
And many other material things.

People became obsessed with
these things
And were led away from the truth.
They struggled through life,

Grew old without ever feeling true happiness,
And died without ever knowing the real God.

This is how they trapped creation
From the beginning of the world until now.

[They took some women and had children in darkness.
They closed their hearts and hardened themselves,
Filling themselves with the false spirit they created,
And this has continued even to this day.]

## The Song of Providence

I am the force that guides everything.
I became like my own children.
I have existed since the beginning.
I have walked every path.

I am the treasure of the light.
I am the memory of wholeness.
I stepped into the deepest darkness and kept going.
I entered the very heart of captivity.
The foundations of chaos shook.

I hid because of their evil,
And they did not recognize me.
I came down again,
Determined to complete my mission.

I rose from among those of the light.
I am the reminder of divine care.
I entered the depths of darkness,
Into the center of the underworld,
To fulfill my purpose.
Once again, the foundations of chaos trembled.

The earth shook violently,
Ready to crumble beneath them,
Threatening to destroy everything.

I rose back into the light,
Returning to my place above,
Choosing to wait before bringing judgment.

Then I descended for the third time.
I am the light.
I live in the light.
I carry the memory of divine care.

I entered the deepest darkness,
The very depths of the underworld.
My face shined with light,
For I knew their suffering would soon end.

I stepped into their prison—
For their bodies were like chains holding them down.
I called out:

Translated by Tim Zengerink

"Wake up!
Rise from your deep sleep!"

The one who had been sleeping awoke,
Tears streaming down,
And cried out:
"Who is calling me?
Where has this hope come from
While I have been trapped here?"

I answered,
"I am the guiding light of divine care.
I am the voice of the Virgin Spirit,
Lifting you to a place of honor.
Stand up!
Remember what you once knew.
Follow the path that leads back to me,
The one who is merciful.

Beware of the demons of poverty.
Beware of the demons of chaos.
Beware of those who seek to keep you trapped.

Wake up!
Stay strong!
Come out of the depths of darkness!"

I lifted him up

And sealed him with the light and water of the five seals.
Death could no longer hold him.

Then I returned to the perfect realm,
Completing my purpose.
And now, you have heard it all.

## Final Message

"I have told you everything,
So you can write it down
And share it secretly with those who truly belong.
This is the great mystery of those who cannot be shaken."

The Savior gave him these words to record and protect.
He warned,
"If anyone trades this truth for gifts,
For food,
For drink,
For clothing,
Or for anything else,
They will be cursed."

These words were revealed to John as a mystery.
Then, in an instant, the Savior disappeared.
John went to his fellow disciples

And told them everything the Savior had shared with him.
Jesus the Christ.

Amen.

# The Reality of the Rulers
# (The Hypostasis of the Archons)

## Introduction

The Reality of the Rulers, known also as The Hypostasis of the Archons, is a profound and fascinating Gnostic text that offers readers an intricate glimpse into the cosmological, theological, and philosophical worldview of early Christian Gnosticism. As part of the Nag Hammadi library—a monumental collection of ancient manuscripts discovered in Egypt in 1945—this remarkable work is among the most significant sources for understanding Gnostic thought, spirituality, and religious imagination in antiquity. The Nag Hammadi texts, comprising codices written primarily in Coptic dating from around the fourth century CE, represent a critical repository of early Christian writings that reveal the richness, diversity, and complexity of spiritual perspectives flourishing alongside, and often in contrast to, mainstream Christianity.

Dating originally from approximately the second or third century CE, The Reality of the Rulers is unique in its portrayal of creation, cosmology, human nature, and salvation. Central to its narrative are the Archons—powerful cosmic rulers depicted as malevolent spiritual entities who exert oppressive control over humanity, trapping human beings within a world characterized by ignorance, suffering, and spiritual blindness. The text vividly narrates the creation of the material world by these inferior divine beings, outlining a distinctive interpretation of familiar biblical stories, particularly from Genesis, thereby revealing a radical reinterpretation of traditional scriptural narratives and theological assumptions.

The purpose of this introduction is to provide readers with a thorough historical, philosophical, and theological framework to deeply engage with The Reality of the Rulers. By understanding its historical origins, exploring its complex symbolism and distinctive cosmological themes, and examining its lasting legacy within religious and philosophical thought, readers will be better equipped to appreciate the richness and profundity of this powerful Gnostic treatise. Through a clear presentation of these foundational contexts, this introduction aims to guide readers toward a more informed and meaningful encounter with the text's profound exploration of spiritual freedom, cosmic power structures, and the human quest for knowledge and liberation.

## Historical and Cultural Background

To fully appreciate The Reality of the Rulers, readers must first understand the historical and cultural milieu in which Gnosticism arose. Gnosticism was a diverse spiritual movement that emerged prominently in the early Christian era, flourishing primarily between the second and fourth centuries CE across various regions of the Mediterranean world, particularly Egypt, Syria, and Asia Minor. Characterized by a profound emphasis on esoteric knowledge ("gnosis") as the key to salvation and spiritual liberation, Gnostic traditions often existed alongside mainstream Christian communities, occasionally provoking intense theological debates and controversies that significantly shaped early Christian orthodoxy.

The Nag Hammadi library, in which The Reality of the Rulers was preserved, represents one of the most significant archaeological discoveries of the twentieth century, providing crucial insights into the rich diversity of early Christian spirituality. Discovered near the town of Nag Hammadi, Egypt, in December 1945, these manuscripts were hidden likely due to rising tensions and the eventual suppression of heterodox spiritual writings deemed heretical by emerging orthodox Christian authorities. The library comprises fifty-two texts across thirteen papyrus codices, dating roughly to the fourth century CE, though most texts, including The Reality of the Rulers, originated much earlier.

Within this complex historical context, The Reality of the Rulers emerged as part of a broader Gnostic discourse concerning spiritual authority, cosmic power structures, and the nature of human existence within the material realm. Gnosticism, in general, offered a radical reinterpretation of biblical narratives, emphasizing the inherent corruption of the physical world, created not by the supreme, transcendent God of pure spirit and light, but rather by ignorant and inferior divine beings (the Archons). This revolutionary cosmological framework profoundly challenged traditional religious understandings, positing a dualistic vision of reality in which spirit and matter existed in fundamental opposition.

Gnostic texts, including The Reality of the Rulers, frequently incorporated and transformed biblical stories, most notably those from the Book of Genesis, to articulate their spiritual insights. They often portrayed conventional religious figures, such as the biblical God of the Old Testament (Yahweh), not as benevolent deities but as misguided or malevolent Archons, whose creation and rule over the material world imprison humanity in ignorance. Such interpretations provided powerful theological critiques of existing religious authority structures, offering alternative spiritual paths emphasizing personal enlightenment, inner wisdom, and liberation from oppressive cosmic powers.

## Cosmological Vision and Theological Themes

At the heart of The Reality of the Rulers lies a deeply imaginative cosmological vision, vividly illustrating the nature, origin, and function of the Archons, who dominate humanity and suppress spiritual awareness.

The text opens dramatically with a reinterpretation of creation, casting the Archons as flawed divine beings mistakenly believing themselves to be supreme creators. Led by the arrogant demiurge Yaldabaoth, who mistakenly proclaims himself the only God, these cosmic powers construct the material world, shaping humanity from dust and imprisoning human souls within physical bodies. Their aim, according to the text, is to obscure true spiritual identity, enforcing ignorance and subjugation through deception, fear, and control.

Central to this cosmological narrative is the theme of spiritual ignorance as humanity's primary plight. The Archons, representing oppressive spiritual powers, maintain their dominion precisely by ensuring human beings remain ignorant of their true divine nature. Gnosticism holds that humanity possesses a hidden spark of divine light—an inner spiritual essence emanating from the transcendent realm of pure spirit, wholly alien to the material cosmos. This divine spark, once recognized through gnosis, grants liberation from Archontic control and reunites the soul with the ultimate transcendent reality. The text's depiction of creation underscores the oppressive and deceptive structures inherent in physical existence, offering a potent critique of worldly authority, material attachments, and conventional religious institutions.

Another significant theological theme within The Reality of the Rulers concerns the role of feminine spiritual figures, particularly Sophia (Wisdom), a central character in Gnostic cosmology. Sophia's actions, often depicted as ambivalent or even rebellious, inadvertently lead to the creation of the Archons, highlighting themes of wisdom, folly, and cosmic tragedy. Yet, Sophia and other feminine emanations also play a crucial role in humanity's redemption, guiding souls toward spiritual awakening, illumination, and liberation. This emphasis on feminine spiritual power provides rich theological symbolism, highlighting divine wisdom, compassion, and liberation as central aspects of Gnostic spirituality.

Additionally, the text reinterprets several key biblical narratives, notably the Eden story, to reveal deeper spiritual truths. Unlike traditional accounts blaming Eve for humanity's fall, The Reality of the Rulers presents the serpent as a liberating figure who encourages humanity to seek knowledge, wisdom, and freedom from Archontic deception. This reinterpretation radically challenges conventional interpretations of biblical texts, emphasizing the pursuit of spiritual enlightenment as humanity's highest calling and necessary rebellion against cosmic oppressors.

## Legacy, Influence, and Modern Significance

The significance of The Reality of the Rulers extends far beyond historical or antiquarian interests. Its profound cosmological insights, radical theological interpretations, and powerful symbolic imagery have significantly influenced religious thought, philosophical inquiry, and cultural imagination across centuries. Historically, Gnostic texts like The Reality of the Rulers profoundly shaped early Christian theological debates, influencing discussions surrounding the nature of God, evil, humanity, and salvation. Though eventually suppressed by orthodox Christianity, Gnostic spirituality continued to influence theological discourse, mysticism, philosophical reflections, and even literary and artistic imaginations throughout subsequent history.

In modern times, renewed scholarly interest in Gnosticism, prompted significantly by the discovery and publication of the Nag Hammadi texts, has profoundly reshaped contemporary understandings of early Christian diversity, spirituality, and cultural complexity. The Reality of the Rulers has attracted attention not only from historians and theologians but also from philosophers, psychologists, cultural theorists, and spiritual seekers intrigued by its deep insights into human nature, spiritual liberation, and cosmic realities. Scholars and readers alike continue to find resonance in the text's potent critique of oppressive structures, its exploration of human spiritual identity, and its call to inner awakening and transformative knowledge.

Today, contemporary interest in Gnostic spirituality reflects broader cultural engagements with themes of spiritual liberation, self-discovery, inner wisdom, and resistance against oppressive power structures—topics deeply resonant within modern religious, psychological, and social discourse. By exploring The Reality of the Rulers, contemporary readers gain powerful insights into ancient spiritual traditions that continue to challenge, inspire, and enlighten modern perspectives.

Ultimately, The Reality of the Rulers stands as a compelling testament to humanity's enduring spiritual quest for knowledge, freedom, and transcendence, offering a provocative vision of cosmic realities that continues to captivate, challenge, and inspire. By deeply engaging with this extraordinary text, readers today encounter profound reflections on spirituality, liberation, and the enduring human struggle against ignorance and oppression, demonstrating the timeless relevance of Gnostic thought and its transformative potential for contemporary spiritual exploration.

## The Reality of the Rulers
## (The Hypostasis of the Archons)

### Samael's Sin

Because of how real these powerful rulers are, and because the spirit of truth guided me, the great messenger explained to us something important about these dark rulers. He told us, "We are not fighting against human beings, but against the powers that rule this world and the evil spirits in it." I'm writing you this because you asked about these rulers.

The leader of these powers is blind. Because he has strength, but also pride and ignorance, he proudly said, "I am God, and there is no one else besides me."

By saying this, he sinned against everyone. His words rose up to the place of purity, and a voice from that place answered him, saying, "You are wrong, Samael," which means "god of the blind."

His thinking became confused. After being thrown out because of his blasphemy, he chased that false power down into chaos and deep emptiness, which is his mother, guided by Pistis Sophia. She made sure that each of his children had a role, based on their power, copying how the higher realms were formed. This is how the visible world was created, using the pattern of the invisible world.

When the pure realm looked down into the waters, her reflection appeared there. The rulers of darkness saw this image and were fascinated by it. But they couldn't grab it, because they were too weak. They had only a soul, not a spirit. The image was from above, and they were from below.

## The Creation of Adam and Eve

This is why the pure realm looked down into the world—to bring everything back to the light, just as the Father wanted.

The rulers made a plan and said, "Let's create a human being from the dirt of the earth." They shaped a man from soil, making him completely from the earth.

These rulers had strange bodies that were both male and female, and their faces looked like wild animals. They took some earth and shaped it into a man, copying their own body and the image of God they had seen in the water.

They said, "Let's trap that image we saw in the water by using the form we made. If we make this man look like it, maybe we can capture it." But they didn't understand the true partner of God, because they were weak. One of them breathed into the man's face, and he became a soul—but he just lay on the ground for many days. They couldn't make him stand up because they didn't have the power. They kept blowing at him like stormy winds, trying to bring that image to life, but they didn't know where its power came from.

All of this happened because the Father allowed it. Later, the spirit saw the man lying there and came down from a strong, heavenly place. The spirit entered the man, and he became truly alive. The spirit named him Adam because he was found moving on the earth.

A voice from the pure place came to help Adam. The rulers brought all the animals of the land and birds of the sky to Adam so he could name them. He gave a name to each one.

Then the rulers put Adam in the garden so he could take care of it. They told him, "You may eat from any tree here, but not from the tree that gives the knowledge of good and evil. Don't even touch it, or you'll die." But they didn't really understand what they were saying. It was actually the Father's plan that Adam would eat from that tree, so he wouldn't see the rulers as if they were just regular people.

The rulers talked again and said, "Let's put Adam into a deep sleep." And he fell asleep. But this "deep sleep" was really ignorance. They opened his side, and something like a living woman came out. Then they filled the space with flesh, and Adam was left with only a soul.

But the spiritual woman came to Adam and spoke to him. She said, "Get up, Adam." When he saw her, he said, "You are the one who gave me life. You will be called 'the mother of the living.'" For she was like a mother to him. She was a healer, a woman, and the one who gave birth.

## Adam and Eve in The Garden

The rulers approached their version of Adam. When they saw the woman with him, they were amazed by her and became very attracted to her. They said, "Let's plant our seed in her," and tried to go after her. But she laughed at them, knowing how foolish and blind they were. Right as they reached her, she turned into a tree and left behind only a shadow of herself. They violated this shadow, not realizing it wasn't truly her. By doing this, they damaged her voice's true expression, and they brought judgment on themselves by using the shape they had created along with their own twisted image.

Then the spiritual woman came in the form of a snake, a teacher. She asked, "What did he tell you? Was it, 'You may eat from every tree in the garden, but not from the one that gives knowledge of good and evil'?"

The physical woman replied, "He said, 'Don't eat from it, and don't even touch it, or you'll die.'"

The snake, still teaching, said, "You won't really die. He said that because he's jealous. If you eat from it, your eyes will open and you'll be like gods, knowing both good and evil." Then the spirit left the snake's form, and the snake became nothing more than a creature of the earth.

The physical woman took fruit from the tree and ate it. She gave some to her husband too, and he ate. These beings only had souls, not spirit, and their flaws became clear. They realized they lacked spiritual awareness and were exposed. So they took fig leaves and covered themselves.

Then the main ruler came and called out, "Adam, where are you?"—he didn't understand what had happened.

Adam answered, "I heard you, and I was scared because I was naked, so I hid."

The ruler asked, "Why did you hide? Did you eat from the tree I told you not to?"

Adam replied, "The woman you gave me handed me the fruit, and I ate it." Then the arrogant ruler cursed the woman.

She said, "The snake tricked me, so I ate." Then they turned on the snake and cursed its shadow, making it powerless. But they didn't realize that it was a shape they themselves had created. From that moment on, the snake was cursed by the rulers until the perfect human would arrive.

Then the rulers took their Adam and his wife and threw them out of the garden. They weren't blessed either, because they were also under the curse.

After that, the rulers distracted people with confusion and hard work, filling their lives with earthly things. They did this so humans wouldn't have time or focus to connect with the holy spirit.

## Eve Bears Children

Later on, Eve gave birth to their son Cain, who became a farmer. He later married and had children. Then she had another son, Abel, who became a shepherd and took care of sheep.

Translated by Tim Zengerink

One day, Cain brought an offering to God from his crops, while Abel offered one of his best young lambs. God accepted Abel's offering but didn't accept Cain's. This made Cain very jealous and angry. He ended up chasing and killing his brother Abel.

Then God asked Cain, "Where is your brother Abel?"

Cain replied, "I don't know. Am I supposed to watch over my brother?"

God said, "Listen! Your brother's blood is crying out to me from the ground. You've sinned by what you did. Your guilt will come back to you. If anyone kills you, they'll be punished seven times over. You'll live a life of sorrow and fear, wandering the earth."

After this, Adam was with Eve again, and she became pregnant and gave birth to another son, Seth. She said, "God has given me another son to take Abel's place."

Eve became pregnant again and had a daughter named Norea. She said, "God has given me a pure daughter to help future generations." Norea remained untouched by the evil forces.

After that, human beings started to grow in number and improve over time.

## The Flood

The rulers made a plan together and said, "Let's cause a great flood with our own hands and wipe out all living things—people and animals alike." But when the leader of the heavenly forces heard about this, he spoke to Noah and said, "Build a boat out of wood that won't rot. Go into it with your children, along with all the animals and birds, from the smallest to the biggest. Place the boat on Mount Sir."

Then Norea came to Noah, asking to get on the boat. But he wouldn't let her. So she blew on the boat and burned it down. Noah then built the boat again, for the second time.

## Norea Battles the Rulers

The rulers came to Norea, trying to trick her. Their top leader said to her, "Your mother Eve came to us."

But Norea replied, "You rulers live in darkness. You are cursed. You didn't know my mother. You only knew your own woman. I don't come from you—I come from the higher world above."

The proud ruler got angry. His face looked like burning fire. He shouted at her, "You must serve us, just like your mother Eve did…"

But Norea stood strong and shouted loudly to the holy one, the true God, "Save me from these evil rulers! Rescue me now from their hands!"

Then a great angel came down from heaven and asked her, "Why are you calling out to God? Why are you speaking so boldly to the holy spirit?"

Norea asked, "Who are you?"

The evil rulers had already pulled back from her. The angel said, "I am Eleleth, the wise one, a great angel who stands with the holy spirit. I've been sent to help you and protect you from the wicked ones. I will also teach you about where you truly come from."

## The Revelation of Eleleth

Now, I can't even begin to describe how powerful that angel was. He shined like pure gold and his clothes were bright like snow. Honestly, I couldn't put into words just how powerful or beautiful his face was.

The great angel, Eleleth, spoke to me and said, "I am understanding. I'm one of the four great lights that stand before the invisible Spirit. Don't worry about those rulers. They have no real power over you. They can't defeat the root of truth. Because of that truth, someone will appear in the last days to stop them. They can't ruin you or others like you, because your home is with the one who can't be corrupted. You belong to the Spirit that's greater than chaos and this broken world."

I said, "Please, sir, explain who these rulers are. Where did they come from? How were they made? Who gave them their power?"

Eleleth, the angel of understanding, said, "The pure Spirit exists beyond everything. Sophia, also called Pistis, tried to create something all by herself, without her partner. What she made was heavenly.

"Between the higher and lower realms, there was a curtain. Underneath it, a shadow appeared. That shadow turned into matter. What Sophia had made fell into this shadowy matter, like a child lost before birth. It turned into a creature made of darkness—a proud beast that looked like a lion. It was both male and female, because it came from matter.

"When it opened its eyes and saw all that matter, it got full of pride and said, 'I am God. There's no one else but me.'

"When he said that, he was wrong. A voice from the highest realm replied, 'You're mistaken, Samael,' which means 'God of the blind.'

"Samael then said, 'If anyone else exists before me, let me see them!' Right away, Sophia pointed her finger and brought light into the matter world. She chased that light into the chaos below, then returned to her own light. Darkness returned to matter.

"This proud ruler, being both male and female, created a huge space for himself. He decided to have children and made seven kids just like himself.

"He told them, 'I am the God of all.'

"But Zoe, Sophia's daughter, shouted back, 'You're wrong, Sakla!'—that's another name for Yaldabaoth. She breathed fire into his face, and that breath turned into a fiery angel that tied up Yaldabaoth and threw him down to the deepest part of the abyss.

"When one of his children, Sabaoth, saw the angel's power, he changed his mind. He rejected his father and mother, who was matter.

"He turned away from them and praised Sophia and her daughter Zoe. Sophia and Zoe rewarded him. They placed him in charge of the seventh heaven, just below the veil between the upper and lower worlds. That's why he's called 'God of the Forces, Sabaoth,' because he's now above chaos. Sophia put him there.

"Then he made a massive chariot with four faces, and filled it with angels, harps, and lyres. It was overflowing with music and light.

"Sophia placed Zoe on his right side to teach him about what's in the eighth heaven. On his left side, she placed an angel of wrath. From that moment on, his right side has meant life, and his left side meant the corruption of the false power above. All this happened before your time.

"When Yaldabaoth saw Sabaoth shining in glory, he became jealous. That jealousy turned into a being that was also male and female. This was the beginning of envy. Envy gave birth to death. Death then had children and gave each of them a place to rule in the heavens. The chaotic skies became filled with them.

"But all of this happened because the Father of all allowed it. It was meant to reflect the higher world and bring the chaos to its end.

"I've now told you how the rulers were made, what they're like, who their parent is, and what kind of world they rule."

\*\*\*

I asked, "Sir, am I made of the same stuff as them?"

He said, "You and your descendants come from the first Father. Your souls come from the pure light above. That's why the rulers can't reach you—because the spirit of truth lives in you. Anyone who knows this path won't die, even though they live in a world full of death. But people won't recognize this truth right away. After three generations, it will be revealed. Then they will be freed from the lies of the rulers."

I asked, "How much longer will it be?"

He replied, "When the true human finally appears in a human body, that's when it will happen. That person will show everyone the spirit of truth sent by the Father.

"He'll teach them everything and anoint them with the oil of eternal life, a gift from a realm without kings.

"They will break free from blindness. They'll overcome death, which came from the rulers, and rise into the endless light where they belong.

"The rulers will give up their control. Their angels will cry over their fall, and their demons will mourn their end.

"Then the children of the light will finally know the truth. They will know their source, the Father of all, and the Holy Spirit. And they will all say together with one voice, 'The Father's truth is right, and the Son rules over all!' And for all time, they will say, 'Holy, holy, holy! Amen!'"

# Allogenes

## Introduction

Allogenes, a compelling yet enigmatic text, stands as one of the profound testimonies to the intricate tapestry of early Gnostic spirituality and metaphysical thought. Discovered among the Nag Hammadi manuscripts in 1945 near the Egyptian town of Nag Hammadi, this document, written in Coptic and originating from an earlier Greek original, offers a captivating insight into a rich and complex religious tradition that flourished in the early centuries of the Common Era. Allogenes invites readers into an expansive journey through the layers of spiritual reality, divine entities, and the mysteries of self-knowledge and redemption. In its cryptic and mystical prose, it echoes the profound quest for understanding and unity with the ultimate divine source that characterized early Gnostic movements.

Gnosticism, broadly speaking, refers to a variety of religious and philosophical traditions that emphasized direct, personal experience and knowledge (gnosis) of the divine. For Gnostics, salvation was not simply a matter of belief or adherence to ritual but involved an inner awakening—a profound realization of one's true origin and nature as inherently divine. Allogenes embodies these principles vividly, presenting its teachings as revelations of esoteric knowledge received by a figure named Allogenes ("the Stranger" or "Alien"), who represents the enlightened seeker who is fundamentally alien to this material world, recognizing his origin in the transcendent realm of the divine.

The text of Allogenes is structured around dialogues, revelations, and visionary experiences that introduce the reader to an elaborate cosmological framework. Central to this framework is the figure known as the "Triple-Powered One," a supreme entity characterized by profound paradoxes: being at once comprehensible and incomprehensible, manifest and hidden, singular and multiple. This figure symbolizes the absolute divine source, from which emanate a series of intermediary divine beings (Aeons) and concepts—such as Barbelo, Protophanes-Harmedon, Autogenes, and Kalyptos—which serve as conduits and reflections of divine energy and knowledge.

The narrative and theological richness of Allogenes reflects its deep roots in a philosophical milieu influenced by Platonic thought, especially the concept of an ineffable and transcendent One. Moreover, it reveals strong ties to broader religious ideas circulating in the Mediterranean and Near Eastern worlds during the second and third centuries CE. These include Jewish mystical traditions, Hellenistic philosophy, and emerging Christian theological speculations. In this sense, Allogenes provides a valuable historical window into the dynamic interplay of cultures, philosophies, and spiritual practices that shaped the early religious landscape.

## Themes and Symbolism in Allogenes: Knowledge, Divinity, and the Path of Enlightenment

A central theme running through Allogenes is the importance of self-knowledge and direct divine revelation as keys to spiritual enlightenment and liberation. Unlike religious traditions that emphasize external authority or adherence to institutional practices, Allogenes insists that true spiritual understanding arises from within—through deep contemplation, visionary experience, and the reception of divine knowledge. It repeatedly stresses the necessity of silence, stillness, and profound introspection as means to encounter the ultimate divine reality.

The Triple-Powered One symbolizes the ultimate unknowable divinity that is beyond all categories and limitations of human thought. This supreme principle is described paradoxically as an "insubstantial substance," a "formless form," and an "inactive activity," emphasizing that conventional human concepts fall short in comprehending the fullness of divine reality. This emphasis on paradox highlights the Gnostic conviction that spiritual truth transcends ordinary logic, inviting the seeker to embrace mystery and ambiguity as essential elements of spiritual growth.

Another vital element of the text is the figure of Barbelo, a central Aeon representing divine forethought and wisdom. Barbelo serves as a mediator between the ineffable One and the material world, embodying the qualities of divine compassion, wisdom, and generative power. Barbelo is depicted as integral to the process of spiritual awakening, guiding individuals toward deeper levels of understanding and inner transformation. In this way, Barbelo represents the compassionate face of the divine, actively involved in humanity's redemption and spiritual ascent.

Throughout the dialogues and revelations, Allogenes stresses the interconnectedness of all existence. The spiritual entities described in the text—Protophanes, Kalyptos, and Autogenes, among others—serve as symbols of spiritual states, levels of consciousness, or modes of divine interaction. These entities illustrate the Gnostic view of the universe as a coherent, interconnected system of spiritual emanations, each playing a specific role in guiding humanity back to its divine origin.

## Contemporary Relevance and the Path of Inner Wisdom

While deeply rooted in ancient religious and philosophical traditions, Allogenes possesses striking relevance for contemporary spiritual seekers. Its emphasis on inner awakening, personal revelation, and self-knowledge resonates strongly in a world often dominated by external distractions and superficial engagements. By advocating for a path centered around deep introspection, mindfulness, and the pursuit of spiritual wisdom, Allogenes offers an enduring invitation to modern readers seeking authentic spiritual insight and personal transformation.

Moreover, the text's depiction of the divine as paradoxically knowable and unknowable challenges contemporary readers to move beyond simplistic notions of spirituality. It invites a contemplative approach to spiritual practice—one that embraces ambiguity, paradox, and the ineffable as vital elements of authentic spiritual experience. This invitation encourages readers to cultivate humility, openness, and a sense of wonder in their spiritual journey.

Finally, the cosmological insights presented in Allogenes offer profound ethical implications. Recognizing the interconnectedness of all existence, and the divine essence that permeates reality, can inspire greater compassion, understanding, and respect for both human and non-human life. By emphasizing the divine potential within each individual, Allogenes encourages readers to approach their lives and relationships with greater care, empathy, and spiritual awareness.

In bringing Allogenes to contemporary readers through this modern translation, we aim to honor the depth, complexity, and beauty of the original text while making its profound teachings accessible and relevant. This translation seeks clarity without sacrificing the mystical resonance and poetic quality of the original, ensuring that readers can engage deeply with the text's rich symbolism and spiritual wisdom.

May your exploration of Allogenes deepen your understanding of the divine, inspire your spiritual journey, and illuminate your path toward the ultimate realization of your inner divine nature and the profound interconnectedness of all existence.

## Allogenes

(5 lines missing)

…since they are complete beings and live together, connected by the mind—the guide I gave you, the one who taught you. This guide is the power inside you. It often speaks as the message from the One with Three Powers. He belongs with the Infinite One, the everlasting Light of Understanding. He is the pure, young male, the first being from the group of eternal beings, coming from a special realm filled with three powers. This Three-Powered-One is truly real. When he became still, he stretched outward. And when he stretched outward, he became complete and received strength from all the others. He understands himself and the perfect Invisible Spirit. He appeared in a realm that knows she understands That One. That realm became Kalyptos, who worked through the ones she understood. He is a perfect, invisible, thoughtful being called Protophanes-Harmedon. She gives power to each person, as the Triple-Male. And even though each person is different...

[5 lines missing]

...they are still united, because she came from them and sees all of them clearly. She holds the divine Autogenes inside her. When she understood her own existence and stood in her power, she brought forth another being, a male, because he saw that all of them existed as individuals, just like he did. And when they become like him, they will see the Triple-Male—the power greater than even God. He is the Thought behind all who exist together. When he thinks about them, he also thinks about the great male being, the thoughtful Protophanes, and their journey. When he sees this, he sees all who truly exist and how they connect. And when he sees them, he sees Kalyptos. If he sees one of the hidden ones, he sees the realm of Barbelo. And as for the child of That One who was never born, if someone understands how he lives...

[4 lines missing]

...then they will understand the richness in each one. Now listen carefully about the invisible, spiritual Triple-Powered-One! He is unseen and beyond their understanding. But he holds all of them within himself, because everything exists through him. He is perfect—more than perfect—and full of blessing. He is always

One and lives in all of them. He can't be described or named. If someone really saw him, they wouldn't care about anything that came before him, because he is the source of all things. He existed before perfection itself. He came before all gods and before all blessings, because he gives power to everything. He's a kind of being that isn't made of anything physical. He's a God greater than any god, whose greatness and beauty go beyond all understanding…

[5 lines missing]

…power. And yet they can come to understand these things, but only if they work together. Since individuals can't fully understand the Universal One who is higher than perfection, they use the First Thought to do so—not just by knowing what "being" is, but by understanding how existence unfolds. He gives everything to himself. He becomes real when he understands who he is. He is the reason everything exists. He is something real without being physical, a number that can't be counted, a form with no shape, a movement that doesn't move, a strength that doesn't force, and action that doesn't act. Still, he provides what is needed. He is the God of all gods. And when people come to understand, they take part in the first Life and a single, united action. This is the foundation of the First One who truly exists. A second action… is the… He is full of blessing and goodness, because when he is known as the one who moves through the endlessness of the Invisible Spirit that lives in him, that endlessness turns back to him. It wants to know what is inside him and how he exists. And he became a savior to everyone by being the starting point for all who truly exist. Through him, knowledge lasted, because he understands exactly who he is. But they created nothing beyond themselves—not power, not rank, not glory, not any realm—because they are eternal. He is Life, Thought, and True Being. Being always contains Life and Thought. Life includes what is not yet understood and Mind. Thought holds both Life and Being. These three are really one, even if they appear different on their own.

When I heard all this, my son Messos, I was afraid. I looked toward the crowd… and a deep thought gave strength to those who were ready to understand these greater truths. And I was able to understand, even though I still lived in a physical body. I heard all this from you, and the teachings within, because the thought inside me could recognize things beyond all limits—even what cannot be known. That's why I'm afraid my teaching might have gone further than it should have.

Then, my son Messos, the glorious being Youel spoke to me again. She revealed something and said:

"No one can hear these truths except the greatest powers, Allogenes. A powerful gift was given to you by the Eternal Father of All, even before you came to this world. It was given so that you could tell apart what is hard to understand, know what most people do not know, and return safely to the One who belongs to you—the One who saved first and does not need to be saved...

[5 lines missing]

...you were shown a form and a vision of the invisible, spiritual Triple-Powered-One. Beyond him is eternal, spiritual knowledge that has no body and can't be divided. Just like the other Aeons, the Aeon of Barbelo also has the shapes and types of those who truly exist—it carries the image of Kalyptos. With the smart, thoughtful Word, he carries the noetic male being, Protophanes, like a reflection. He acts within people through skill, talent, or even natural instinct. He carries the divine Autogenes like an image and understands each one. He works separately and personally with each being, helping fix what nature could not finish. He carries the divine Triple-Male to bring salvation to all, working together with the Invisible Spirit. He is a Word that comes from wisdom. He is the perfect Youth. And this being...

[6 lines missing]

...made my soul grow weak. I ran away and was deeply shaken. But then I turned inward and saw the light that surrounded me and the Goodness that lived inside me—and I became divine. The all-glorious One, Youel, anointed me again and gave me power. She said:

"Since your learning is now complete, and you have found the Good within yourself, listen to what I say about the Triple-Powered-One. Keep this in great silence and mystery. These truths are only for those who are worthy—those who are able to hear. They must not be spoken to those who are unprepared. It is not right to share knowledge about the Universal One, who is higher than perfection, with people who aren't ready. But you have received all this because of the Triple-Powered-One—the One who lives in blessing and goodness, the One behind all things.

"There is great greatness within him. Even though he is One...

[5 lines missing]

...he came from the First Thought, which always stays with those who have true understanding. That One moved without moving, staying still in what is in control, so he wouldn't fall into the endless by being pulled by another thought. He turned inward and revealed himself, containing everything—the Universal One who is greater than perfect.

"It's not through me that he is so far beyond knowledge. Even though no one can fully understand him, he can still be known. This is possible because of the third silence of Mind and the second united action, which appeared in the First Thought—that is, the realm of Barbelo—along with the Indivisible One, the Triple-

Powered-One, and the being that isn't made of anything physical."

Then a power appeared in a way that was completely still and silent—but it made a sound like "zza zza zza." And when she (Youel) heard this sound, she was filled…

[5 lines missing]

"You are […], Solmis! … through your Life and your first divine action. You are great, Armedon! You are perfect, Epiphaneus!

And through your second power and your Thought from blessing:

Autoer, Beritheus, Erigenaor, Orimenios, Aramen, Alphleges, Elelioupheus, Lalameus, Yetheus, Noetheus—

you are great! Anyone who knows you knows the Universal One!

You are One—you are the Good One, Aphredon!

You are the Eternal Aeon of Aeons!"

Then she praised the Universal One and said:

"Lalameus, Noetheus, Senaon, Asineus, …riphanios, Mellephaneus, Elemaoni, Smoun, Optaon—

You Are! You are the One Who Is, the Aeon of Aeons, the One never born, greater than the unborn!

Yatomenos, you alone are the reason the unborn were born!

You are the One who cannot be named!"

[10 lines missing]

…knowledge."

After I heard all these things, I saw the glory of the perfect beings—the ones who are fully complete and live together—and the even greater ones who came before them.

Here is your passage translated into simpler, clear English suitable for an 8th-grade reading level. The structure is preserved, including all original [missing lines] placeholders and dialogue rendered in natural, modern speech.

*** 

Then the glorious being Youel said to me again, "Allogenes, even if you don't fully understand, you still know that the Triple-Powered One existed before all greatness. These powers don't exist among the usual beings. They're not part of what exists in the normal way or even with those who truly exist. Instead, they exist as divine, blessed, and real—but also as something without physical substance or ordinary existence."

Then I prayed to receive a revelation. And the all-glorious Youel said to me, "Yes, Allogenes, the Triple-

Male is beyond physical matter. But even though he has no form...

[9 lines missing]

...he exists with those who come from the true, eternal beings. The self-born ones are with the Triple-Male.

"If you search sincerely, with everything in you, you'll discover the Good that lives within you. Then you'll recognize who you really are—someone who comes from the God who existed before all. A hundred years from now, you will receive a revelation of that One, through Salamex, Semen, and the shining lights of Barbelo's realm. But you won't understand things that go beyond your ability, at least not right away, so you don't lose your place among your kind. But when you do begin to understand That One, then you'll be filled with truth completely. That's when you'll become divine and complete. You'll receive...

[4 lines missing]

...what you've been looking for. This Existence—if it understands anything, it's through the one doing the understanding and the one being understood. And when that happens, the one who understands becomes greater than the one being understood. But if that person drops back into their natural state, they become smaller, because the ones without bodies don't exist in terms of size. They have a kind of power that lets them be everywhere and nowhere at once. They are bigger than anything measurable and smaller than anything tiny."

After Youel finished speaking, she left me. But I didn't give up on the words she shared. I stayed with them, thinking about them deeply for a hundred years. I was filled with joy because I was surrounded by light and walking a blessed path. I had been allowed to see and hear things that only the great powers should witness...

[5 lines missing]

...from God.

As the hundred years came to an end, I received a blessing of eternal hope, full of peace. I saw the good, divine Autogenes. I saw the Savior—the youthful, perfect Triple-Male Child. I saw his goodness, the wise and complete Protophanes-Harmedon. I saw the joy of Kalyptos. I saw the source of all that joy: the divine realm of Barbelo. And I saw the origin of the one who has no beginning—the spiritual, invisible Triple-Powered One, the Universal One who is greater than perfection.

I was lifted out of my physical body by the eternal Light and taken to a sacred place that no one in the world could imagine. There, surrounded by deep joy, I saw all the beings I had heard about. I praised them all. I stood on the foundation of what I had come to know, and I turned toward the understanding of the great realm of Barbelo.

I saw sacred powers through the light of the pure male Barbelo. They told me I would be able to understand how the world works:

"Allogenes, see the blessing within you, how it quietly stays with you. Through it, you understand your true self. And in seeking that, you'll return to the Life-force within, which you'll see moving. Even if you feel like you can't stay upright, don't be afraid. But if you want to remain strong, return to your true Existence. There, you'll find it standing still—just like the One who is always at rest and silently embraces all things.

"When you receive a first glimpse of the Unknown One—if you try to understand him, become unaware of him again. And if you become afraid in that place, take a step back from all the activity. Once you are complete there, be still. The pattern that lives inside you is how all things work. Don't scatter your energy, so you can remain standing. Don't try to act too much or you'll lose touch with the quietness of the Unknown One. Don't try to fully know him—it's not possible. But if your enlightened thought tries to understand him, become unaware again."

I was quietly listening to these words. Inside me, there was total stillness, and in that silence, I heard the blessing that helped me realize who I really am.

I turned inward to the Life-force I had been seeking, and I joined with it. I stood—not firmly, but calmly. I saw an endless, thoughtful movement that connects all the shapeless powers. It had no limits and was free from anything fixed.

When I tried to stand firmly, I returned to true Existence. I found it standing still, like a reflection of what had been revealed to me by the Indivisible One, the One who is always at rest. I was filled with a vision from the Unknown One. Though I couldn't understand him fully, I somehow knew him. And through him, I gained power. Now stronger, I knew the One who lives inside me, the Triple-Powered One, and his ungraspable nature. Through the first revelation of the First One, who is unknown to all, I saw him—and the Triple-Powered One who lives in all beings. I was searching for the God beyond understanding—the one who, if someone thinks they understand him, proves they do not. He is the guide between us and the Triple-Powered One. He is peaceful and silent, but unknown.

Once I was firm in this understanding, the great lights spoke again:

"Stop disturbing the stillness within you by chasing what can't be grasped. Instead, listen—understand him as much as possible through your first vision and through revelation.

"He is what he is because he exists, or will exist, or acts, or understands. But he doesn't live with mind, or life, or existence—or even non-existence. He exists alongside himself. He's not something left over or something that gets purified or shared. He doesn't shrink or grow. He doesn't want anything—not from himself or from anyone else. He doesn't give things away to avoid losing something. He doesn't need mind or life or to 'be' anything at all. He's above even the highest truths because of his silence and stillness. These protect him from being changed or reduced by anything.

"He is not a god, or joy, or perfection—though those things are related to him. He's something even higher. He's not perfection itself but beyond it. He's not endless or limited—just beyond. He's not a body or without one, not large or small, not a number or a thing created. He's not something we can know. He's something totally different, and we can't understand him.

"He knows himself and is the only one who truly does. He's not like anything else. He's above all words—even words that describe things that can't be described. He doesn't exist within time or age. He doesn't take anything from anything. He can't be reduced, and he doesn't reduce anything. He knows himself, beyond what even the most unknowable beings could imagine.

"He carries joy, perfection, silence, and stillness—not those things exactly, but something beyond them that no one can understand. These are just parts of what he is. He's more beautiful than anything good, and no one can understand him in any way. He lives within everything, even though no one can truly know him.

"If someone says they understand him—or thinks of him as knowledge itself—they're wrong. They've misunderstood God. And their own failure to see truth will be their punishment—not because God punishes, but because they missed the true beginning. They were blind without the eye of revelation, the one that rests in the power of the Triple Thought from the Invisible Spirit. This eye exists from...

[15 lines missing]

...something rooted in pure beauty and peaceful silence—unshakable and beyond all imagining. When he appeared, he didn't need time, and he didn't belong to eternity either. He is completely beyond understanding. He doesn't need to do anything to find peace—he already is peace. He isn't something that exists because that would mean he lacks something. In physical space, he might seem to have a form, but truly, he doesn't. He exists beyond being and doesn't want anything. He is the highest peak of greatness, higher even than stillness itself, so that...

[15 lines missing]

...he saw them and gave them strength, even though they don't focus on him at all. And even if someone receives something from him, it isn't power as we know it. He can't be affected. He is unchanging unity. He is beyond knowing—like a space without air, beyond limits. He didn't create existence, but holds it within himself. He stays at rest and is connected to the one who always stands firm. From him came Eternal Life—the Invisible and Triple-Powered Spirit—who lives in all that exists and surrounds everything. It is above all...

[15 lines missing]

...he was filled with strength. He stood among them, empowered them all, and filled them completely."

You've heard all these things. Don't look for more. Just go. We don't know if the Unknown One has angels or gods or anything inside himself besides stillness. That stillness is him. If we keep searching too much, we risk going too far. What you were meant to know has been revealed. Others will speak with someone else. But you will receive them...

[5 lines missing]

...Then he said to me, "Write down everything I'm about to tell you. Save it for the ones who will be ready after you. Leave the book on a mountain and call out to its guardian: 'Come, Fearsome One.'"

After saying this, he left me. But I was filled with joy. I wrote this book just as he told me to, my son Messos. I wanted to pass on everything that had been revealed to me. At first, I received it all in complete silence. I stood alone and prepared myself. These are the things that were shown to me, my son Messos...

[13 lines missing]

...Share these words, my son Messos, as the final message that completes all the writings of Allogenes.

# Thank You for Reading

Dear Reader,

We hope this timeless classic has sparked your imagination and enriched your literary journey. Now that you've turned the final page, we want to share a vision for the future of reading—one where every classic you've ever wanted to explore is at your fingertips, in a format that best suits your life.

We'd like to invite you to gain immediate, unlimited digital & audiobook access to hundreds of the most treasured literary classics ever written—along with the option to secure deluxe paperback, hardcover & box set editions at printing cost. Together, we can spark a new global literary renaissance alongside our small, independent publishing house called "The Library of Alexandria."

Thousands of years ago, the Library of Alexandria stood as a beacon of knowledge—until it was lost to history. We aim to reignite that spirit of preservation and discovery right now, in the modern age—only this time, it's accessible to all, in every language and every format.

Picture a world where every timeless classic, novel, poem, or philosophical treatise is not only available to read but also updated for today's readers—modernized, translated into any language or dialect, and ready to enjoy in any format you choose, whether that is in an eBook, audiobook, paperback, or deluxe hardcover & box set version a printing cost.

By joining our movement to rebuild the modern Library of Alexandria, you become part of an unprecedented mission to offer:

- **Unlimited Audiobook & eBook Access to the Greatest Classics of All Time**

  Instantly explore thousands of legendary works, from Plato and Shakespeare to Jane Austen and Leo Tolstoy. All are instantly ready to read or listen to, giving you a complete literary universe at your fingertips.

- **Paperback & Deluxe Editions at Printing Costs:**

  Purchase any title in a paperback, deluxe hardbound, or deluxe boxset edition at printing costs, shipped right to your doorstep. Curate your personal library of Alexandria with editions worthy of display—crafted to last, designed to captivate, and delivered straight to your door.

- **Modern translations for Contemporary Readers in all languages and dialects**

  Discover a vast selection of classics reimagined in clear, current language—no more struggling with outdated phrases or obscure references. Next to the original versions, we aim to offer translations in as many languages and dialects as possible.

As we continue our translation efforts and add new languages, readers everywhere can connect with these works as if they were written today. By bridging linguistic divides, you're contributing to ensuring that these timeless stories become more meaningful, accessible, and inspiring for people across the globe.

- **Your Personal Library of Alexandria:**

Over the months and years, you'll curate a unique physical archive of classics—each volume a testament to your taste, curiosity, and love of knowledge. It's not just about owning books—it's about curating a cultural legacy you'll cherish and pass down for generations to come.

- **Join a Global Literary Renaissance:**

Your support fuels an ongoing mission: allowing us to reinvest in offering deluxe print editions (including special boxsets) at their true cost, broaden the range of available formats and translations, and extend the reach of these works to new audiences worldwide. By joining today, you're not just preserving a legacy of masterpieces; you set in motion a powerful wave of literary accessibility.

We are more than a publisher—we're a movement, and we can't do it alone. Your support lets us scale our mission, preserving and reimagining history's greatest works for tomorrow's readers.

**Become a Torchbearer of knowledge.**

Thank you for picking up this book and allowing us into your literary journey. As you turn the pages, know that you're part of something larger: a global effort to keep these stories alive, share their wisdom across borders and generations, and spark a true cultural revival for the modern era.

If this resonates with you—please consider taking the next step by visiting:

**www.libraryofalexandria.com**

With gratitude and a shared love of knowledge,

The Modern Library of Alexandria Team

Visit:

www.libraryofalexandria.com

Or scan the code below:

www.ingramcontent.com/pod-product-compliance
Lightning Source LLC
LaVergne TN
LVHW030630080426
835512LV00021B/3443